I0510347

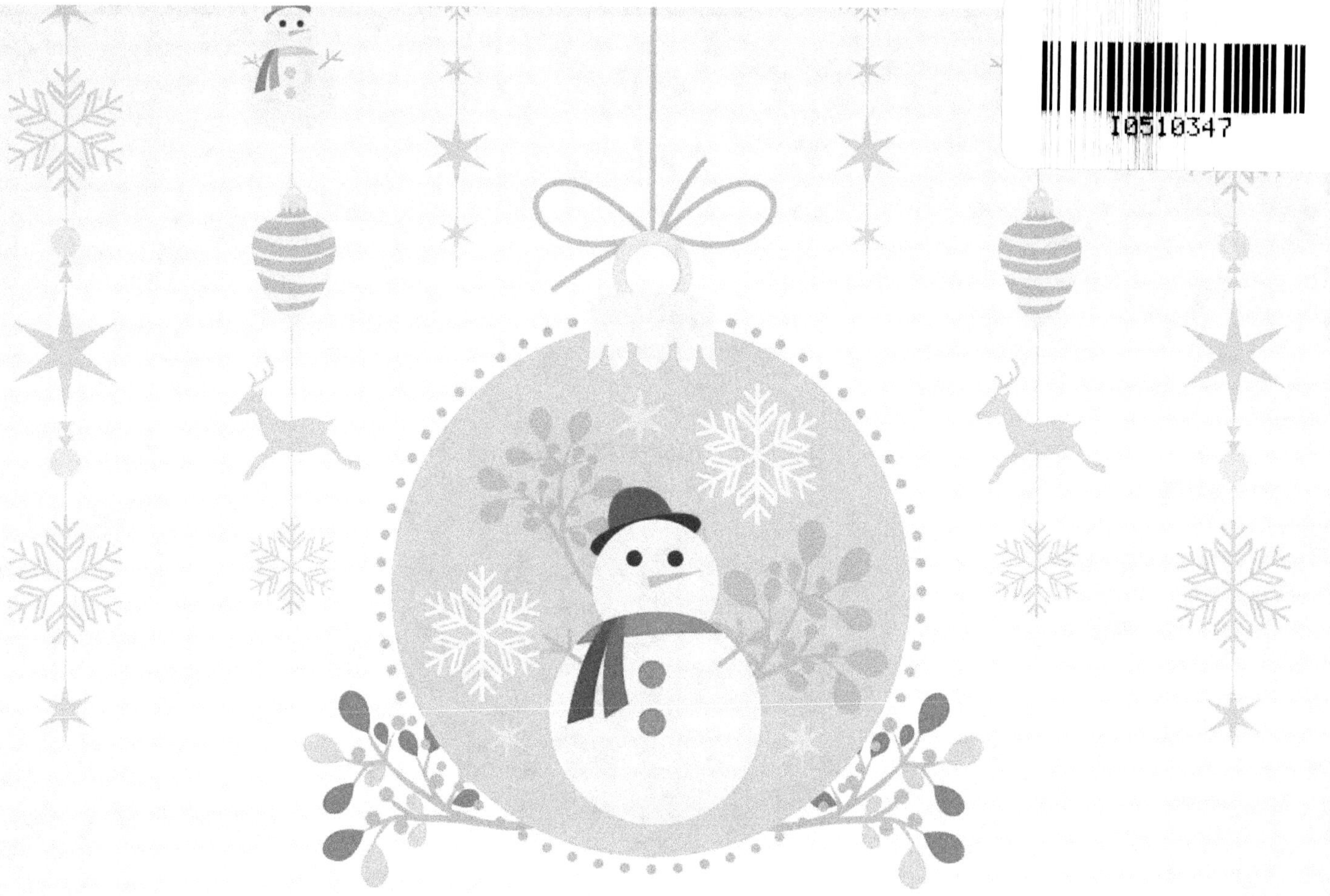

# Merry
# CHRISTMAS

## This Books Belongs To

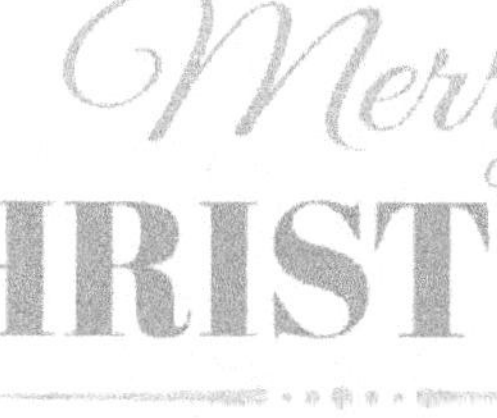

.......................................................

.......................................................

.......................................................

.......................................................

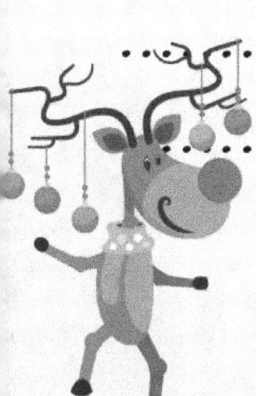
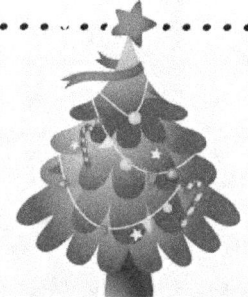
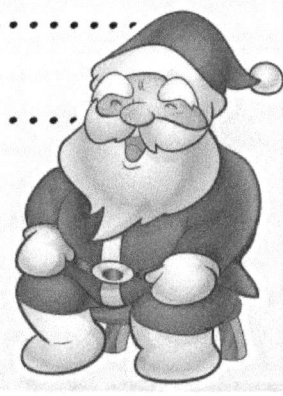

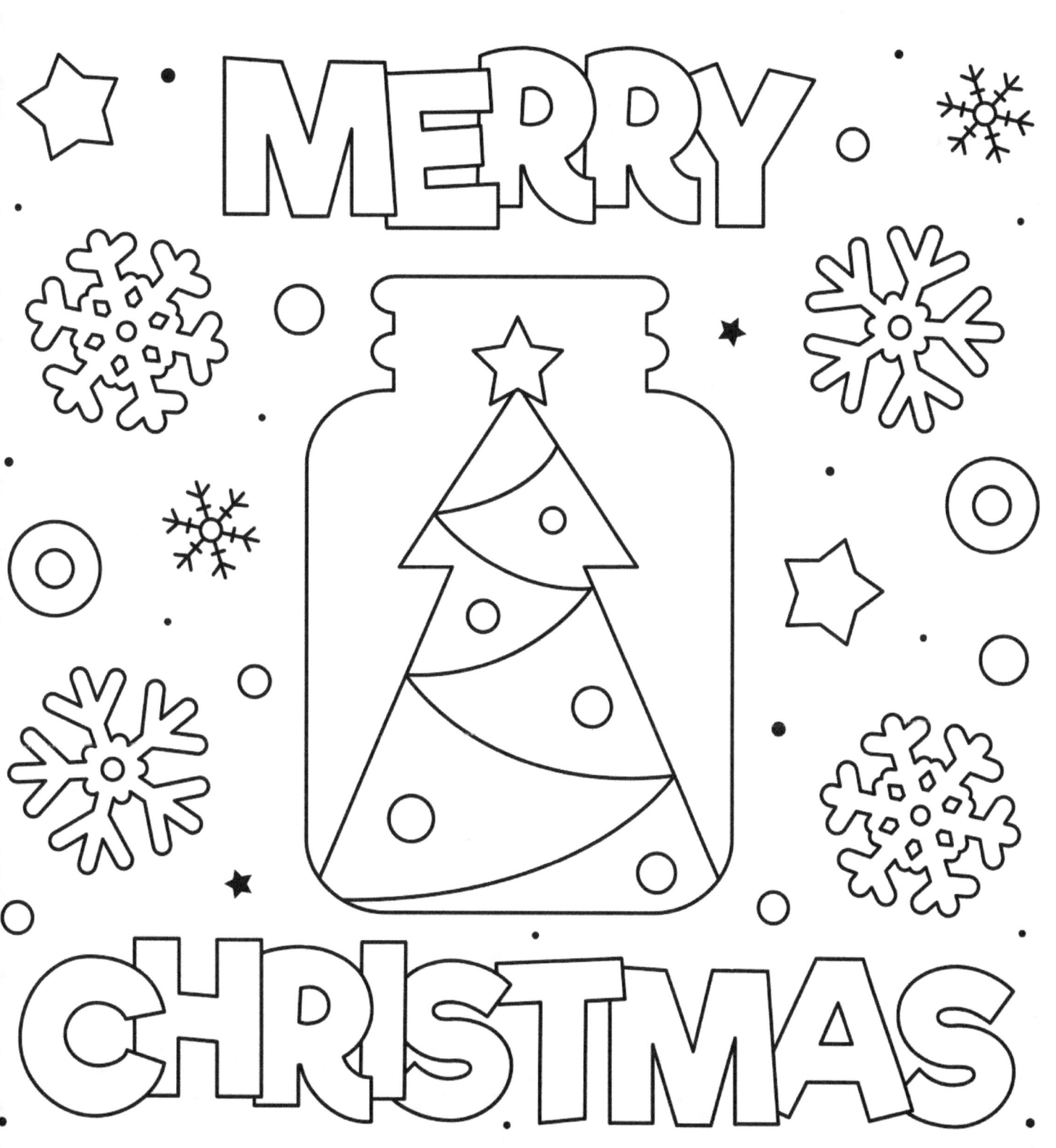

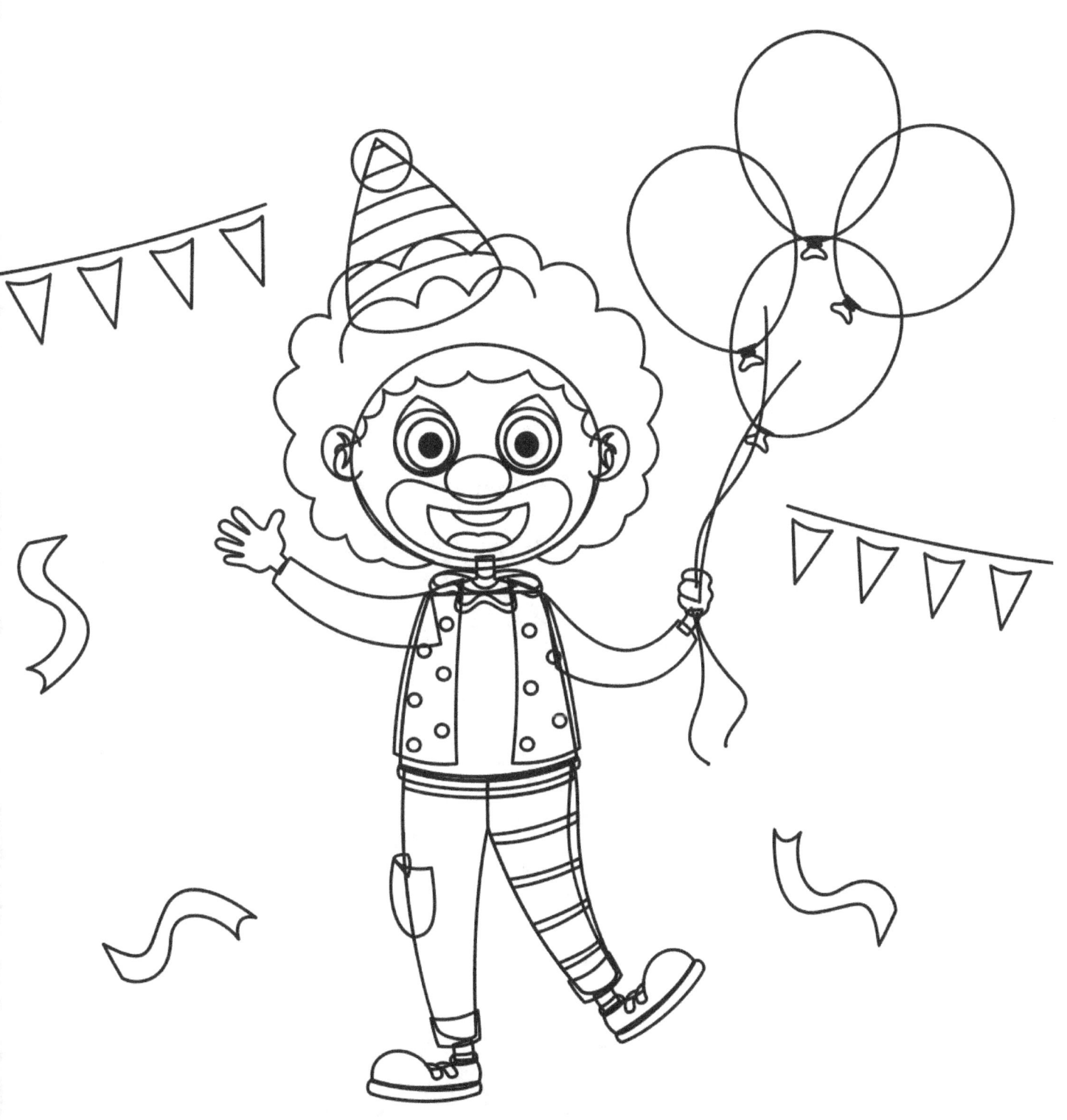

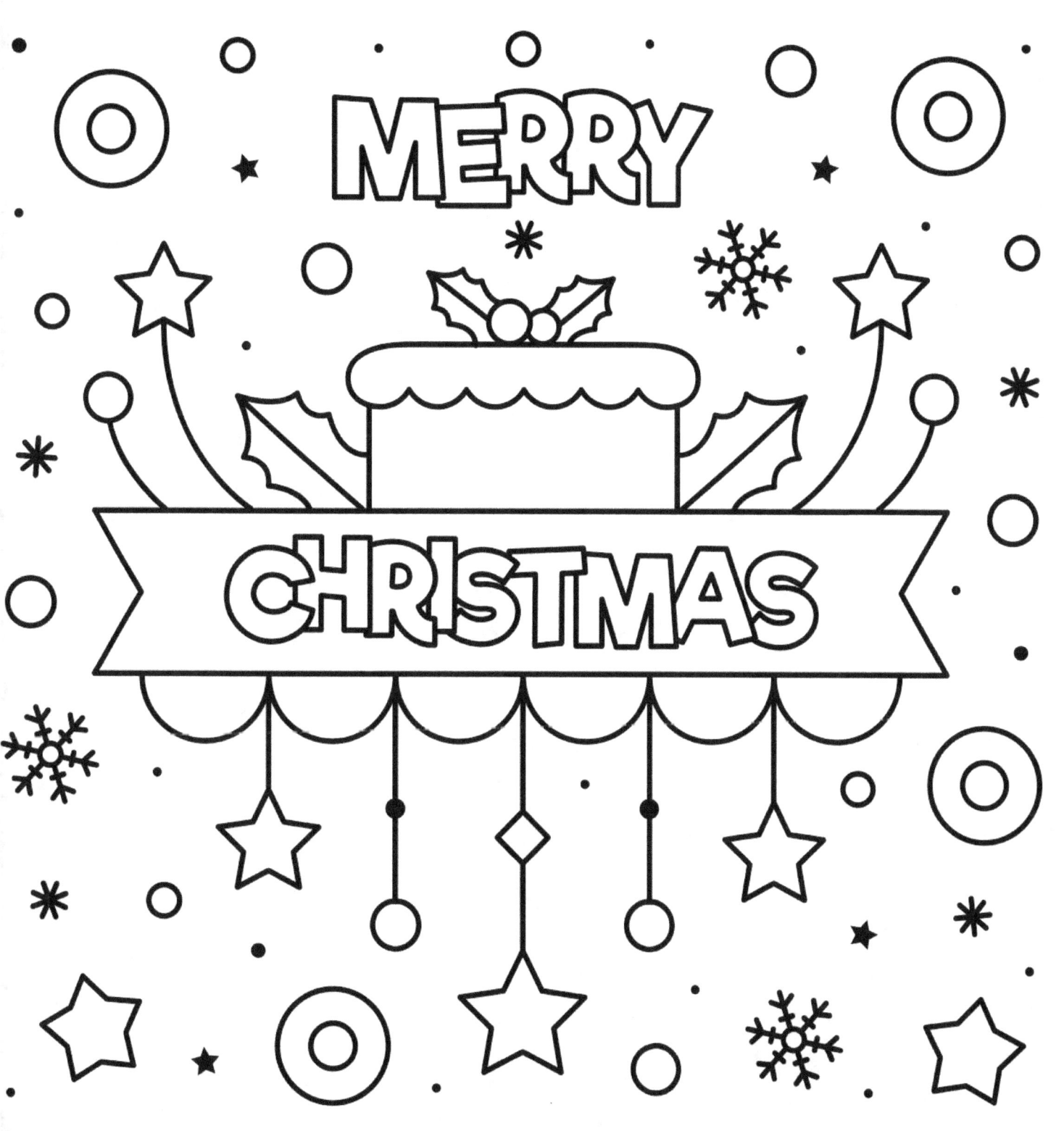

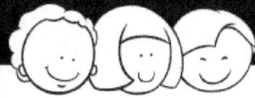

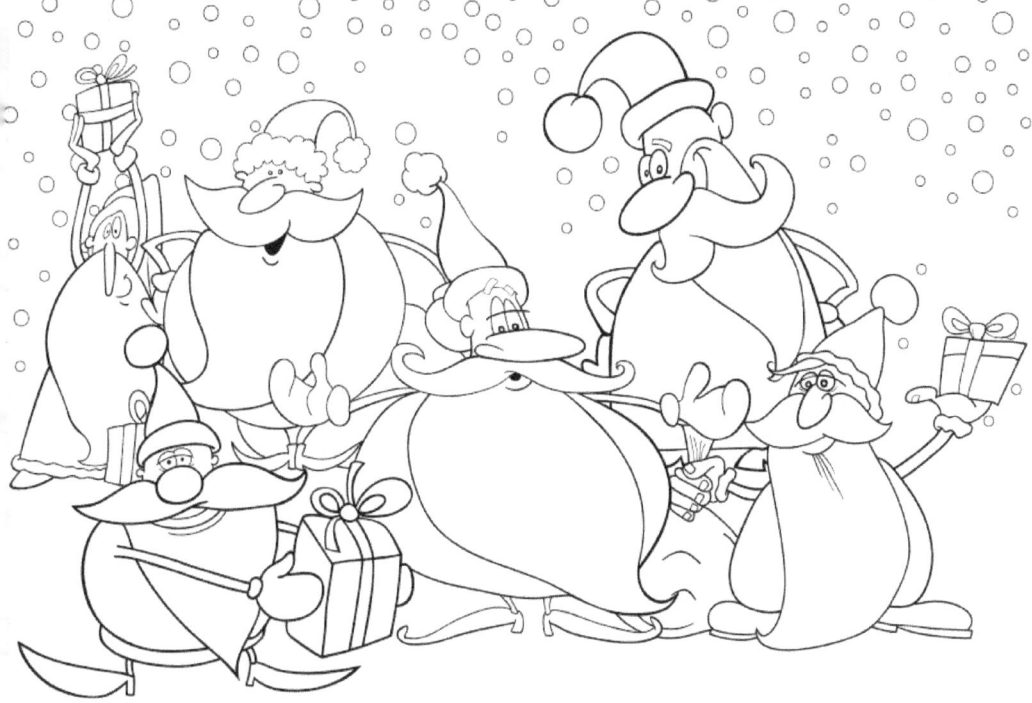

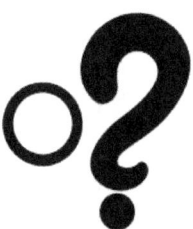

FIND
**7**
DIFFERENCES

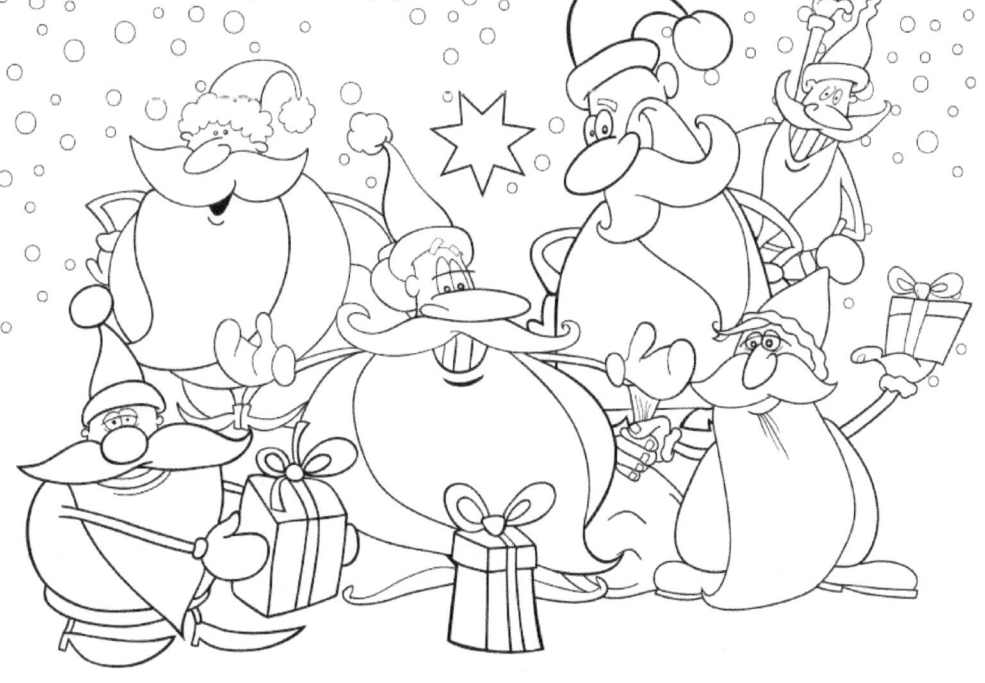

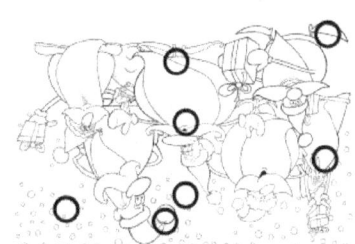

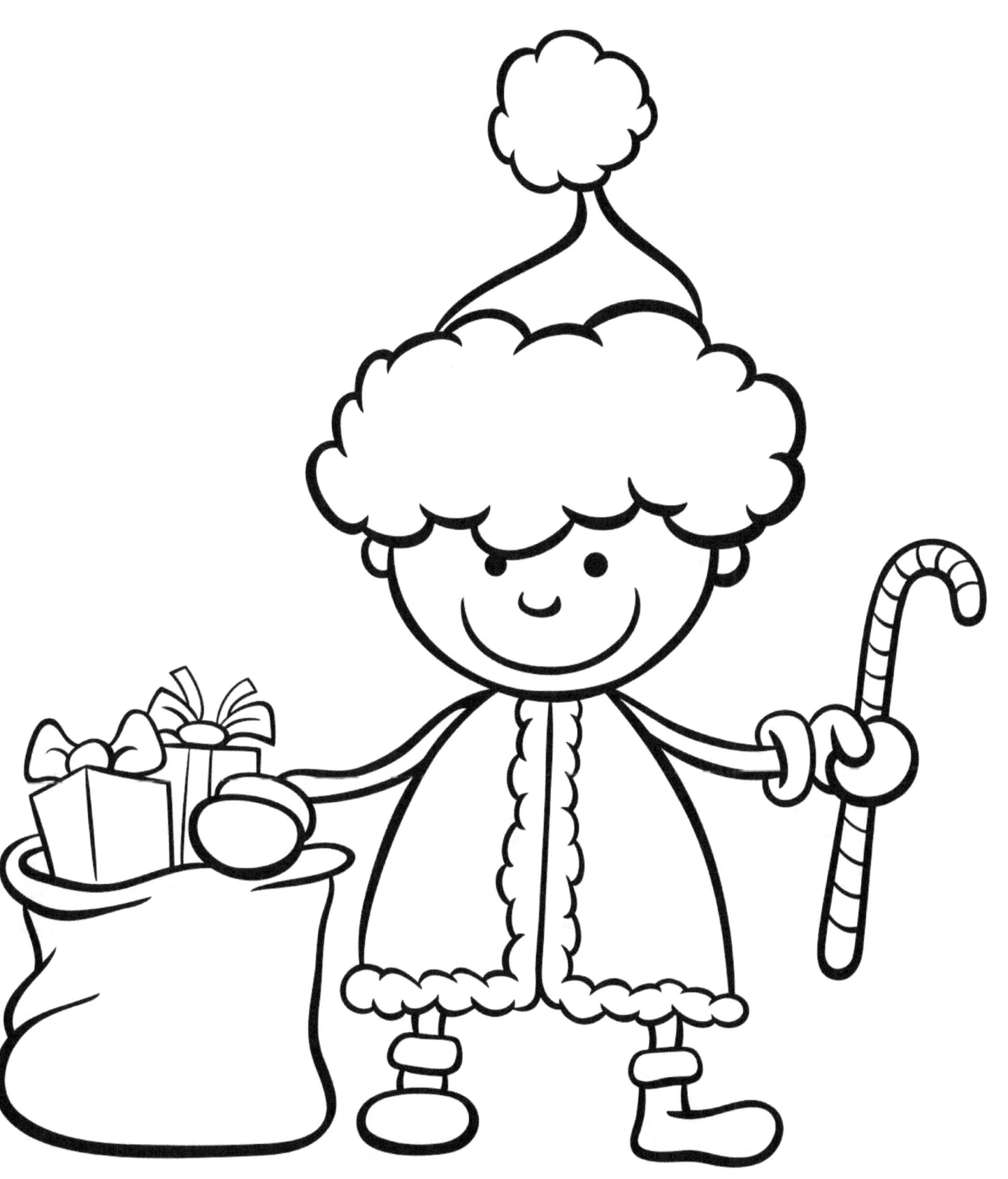

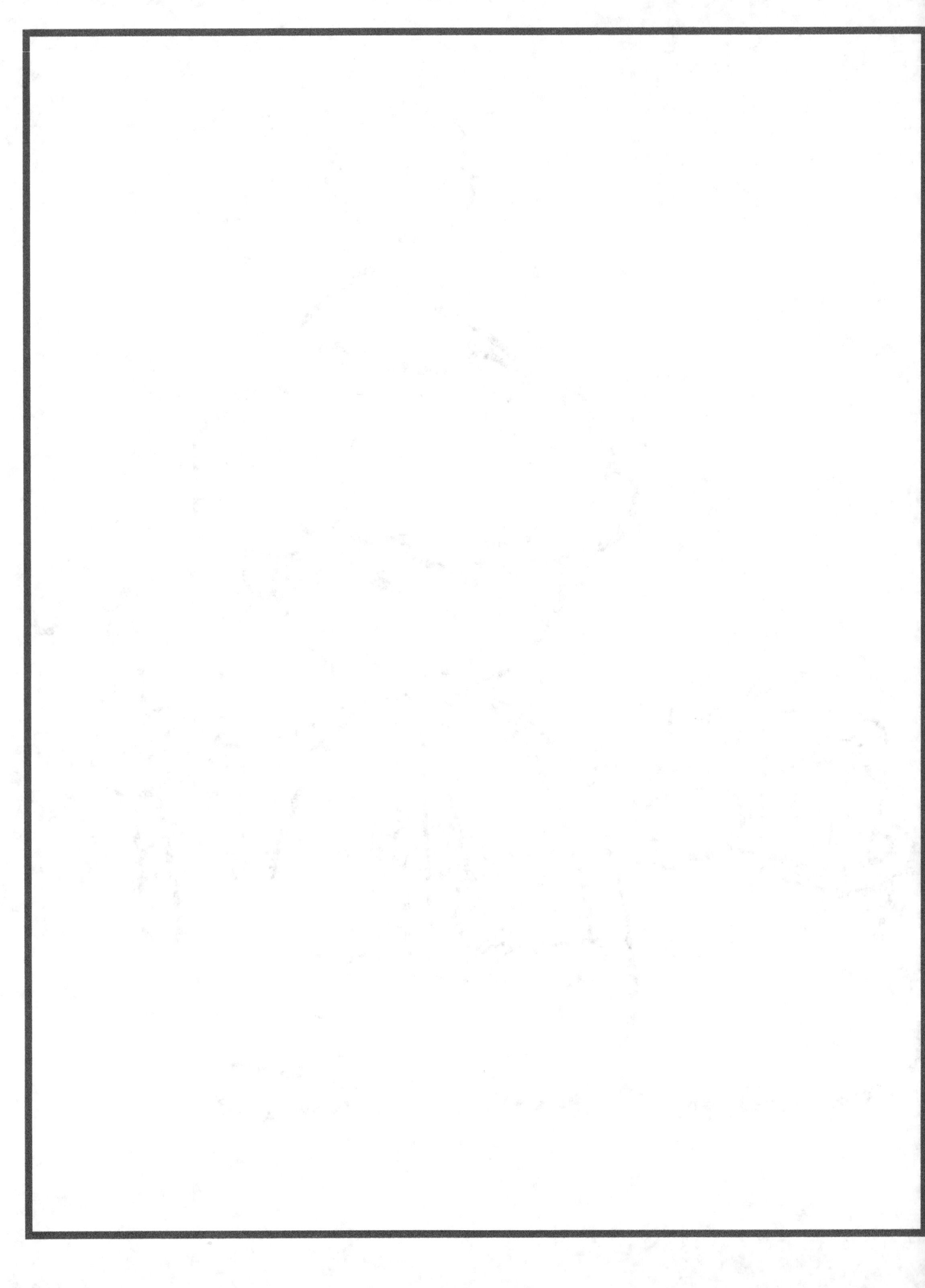

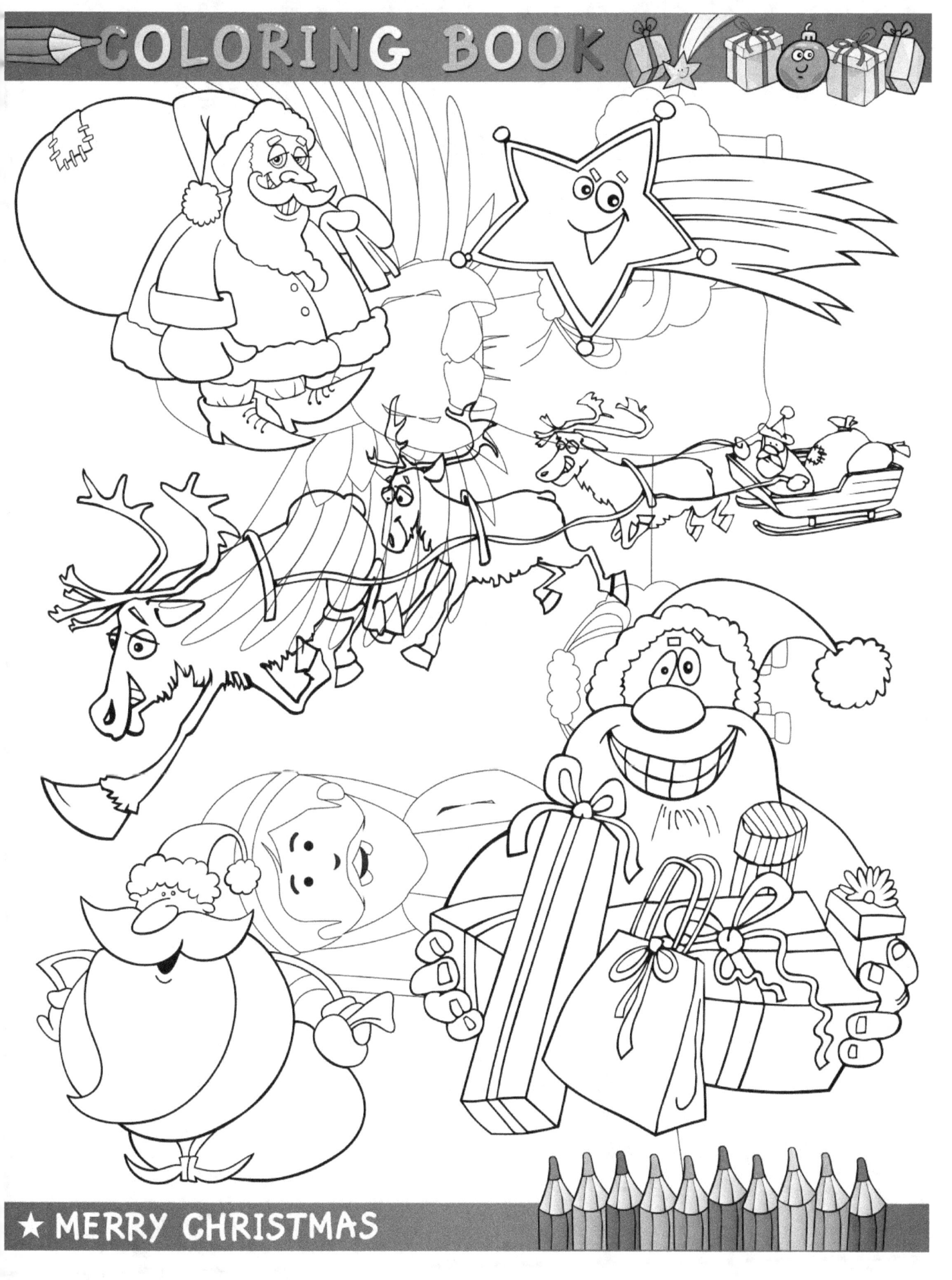

# COLORING BOOK

★ MERRY CHRISTMAS

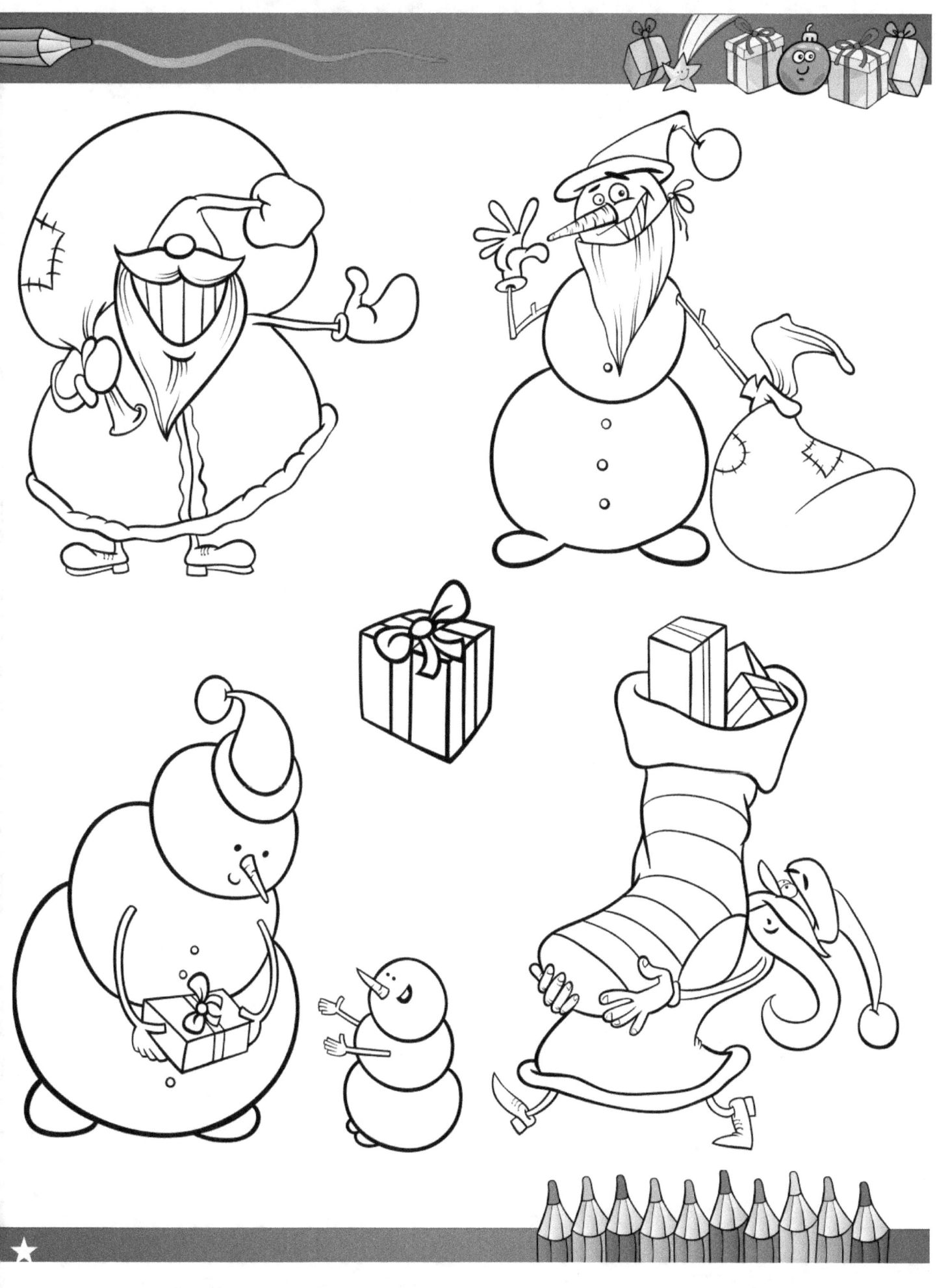

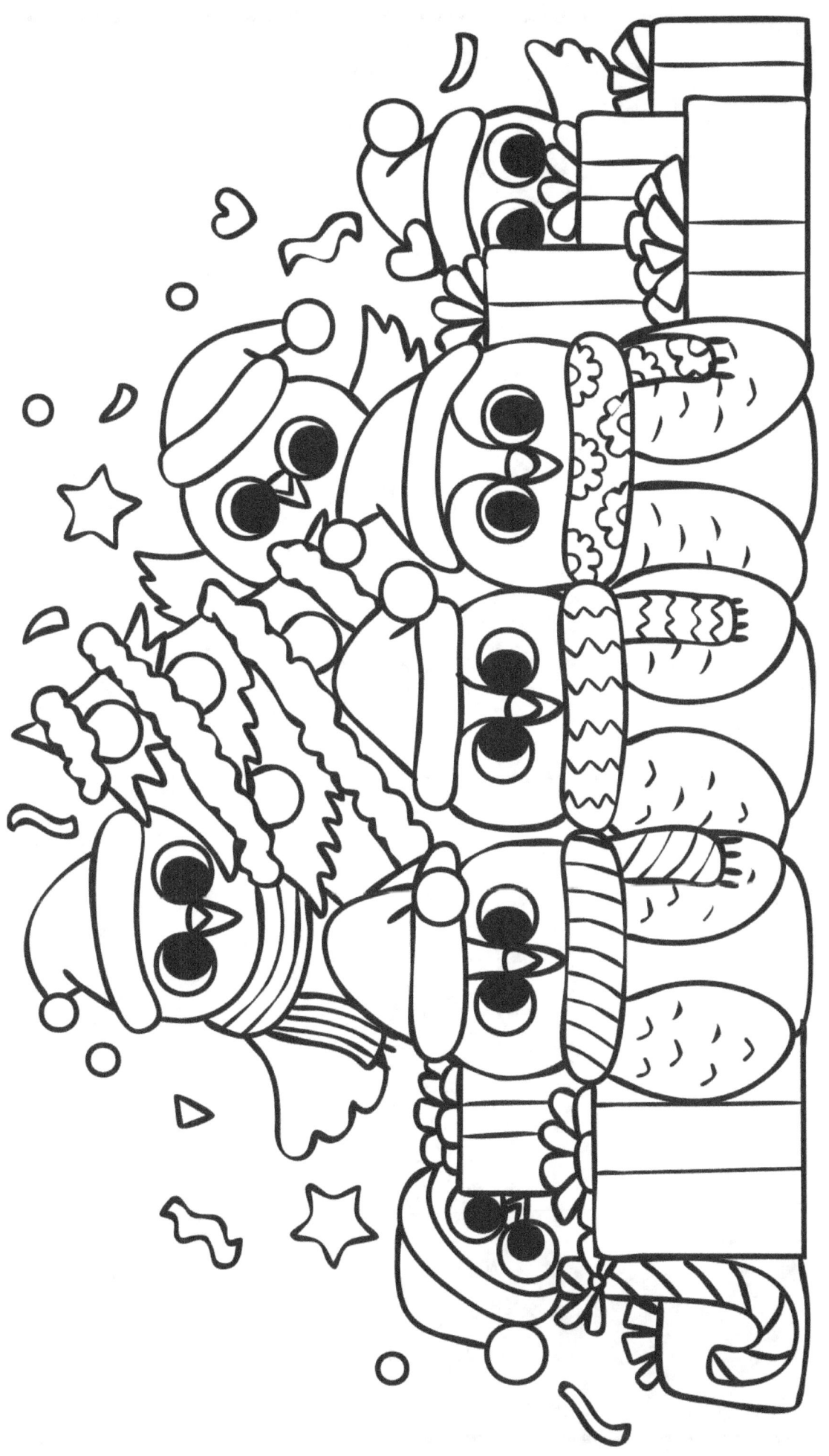

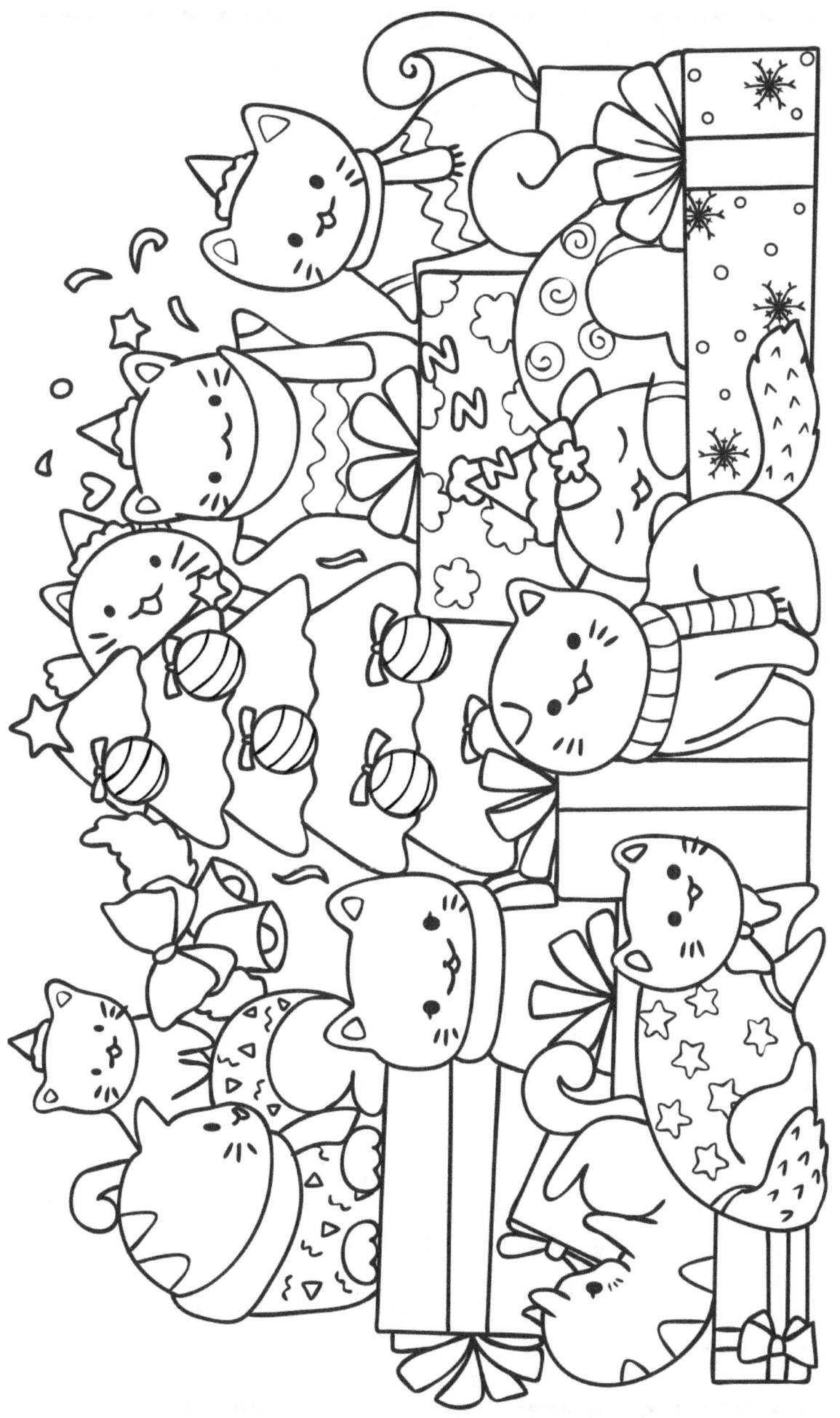

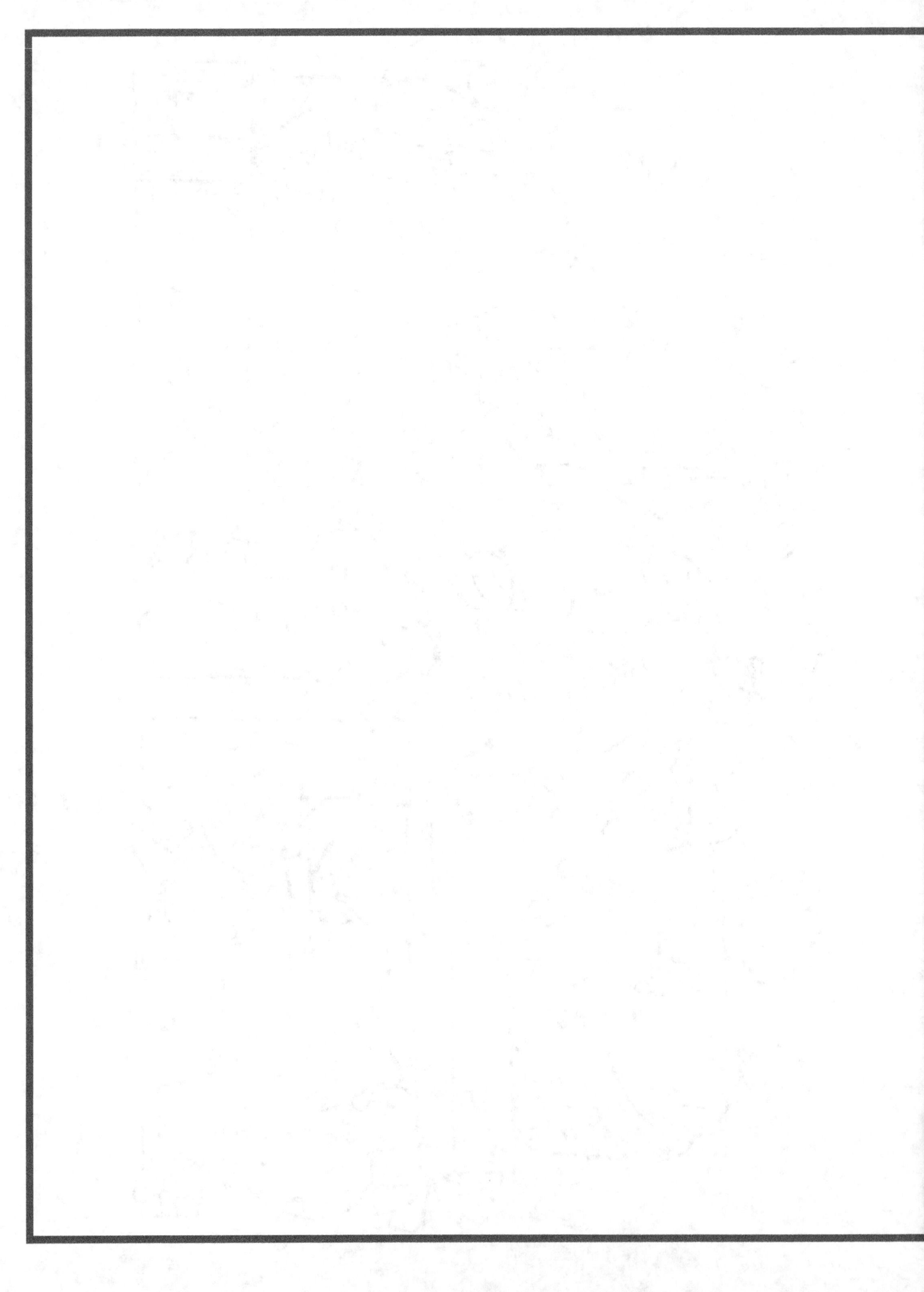

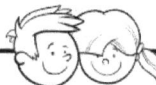
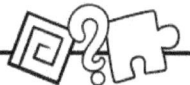

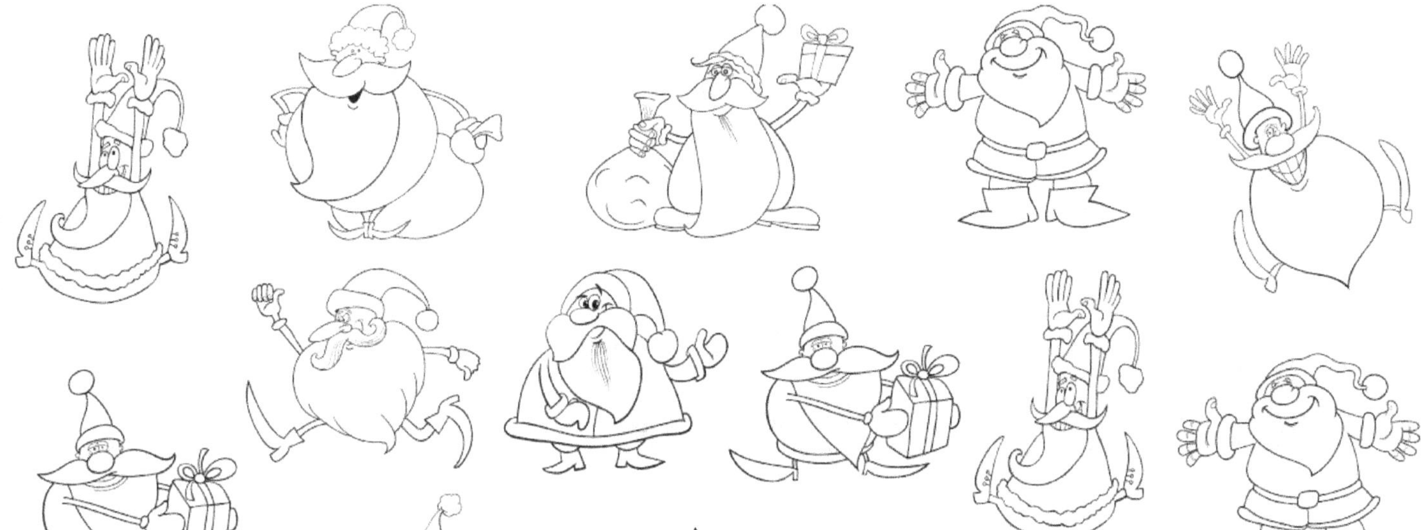

# CHRISTMAS

## FIND
## ONE
## OF A KIND

ANSWER

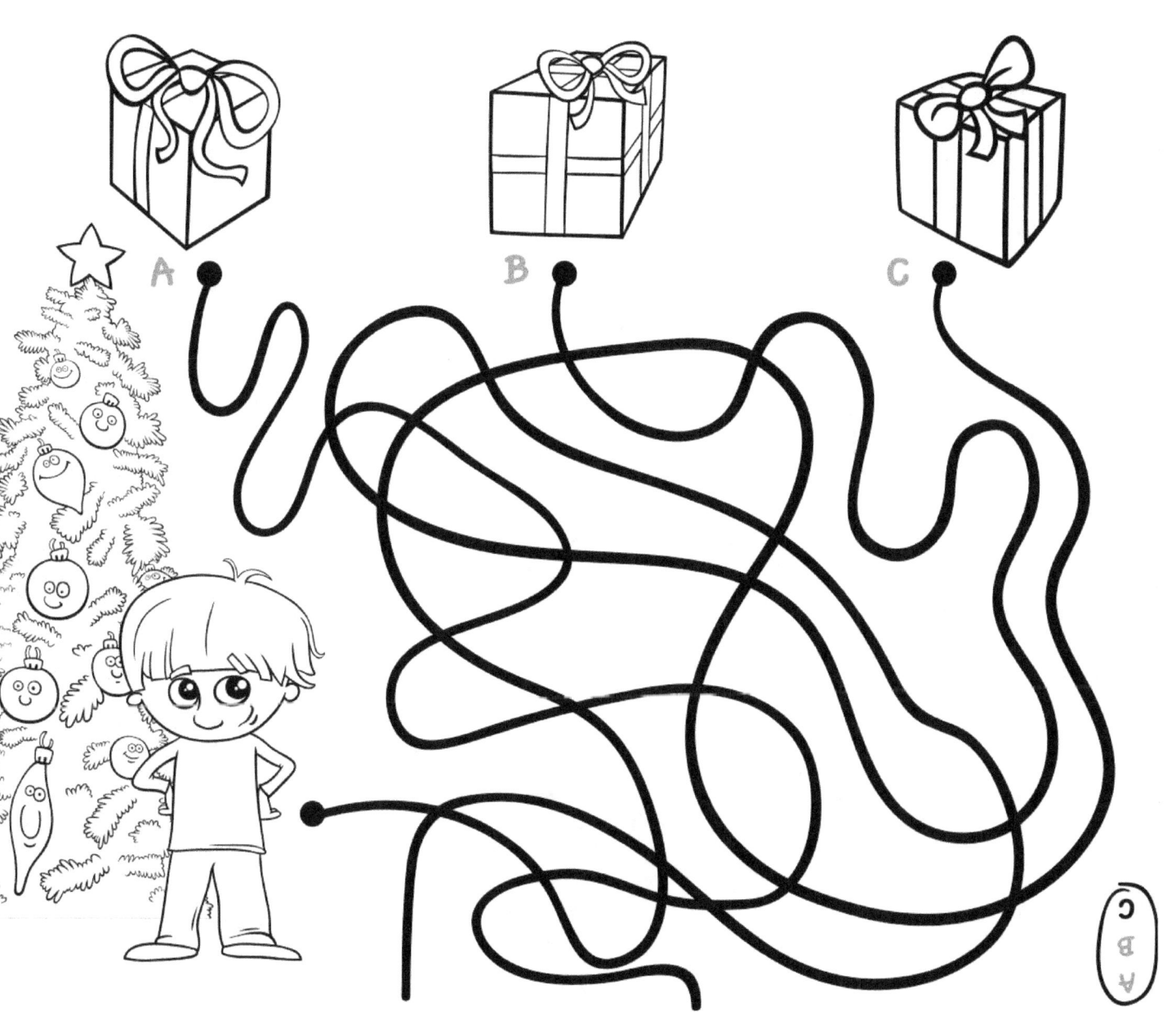

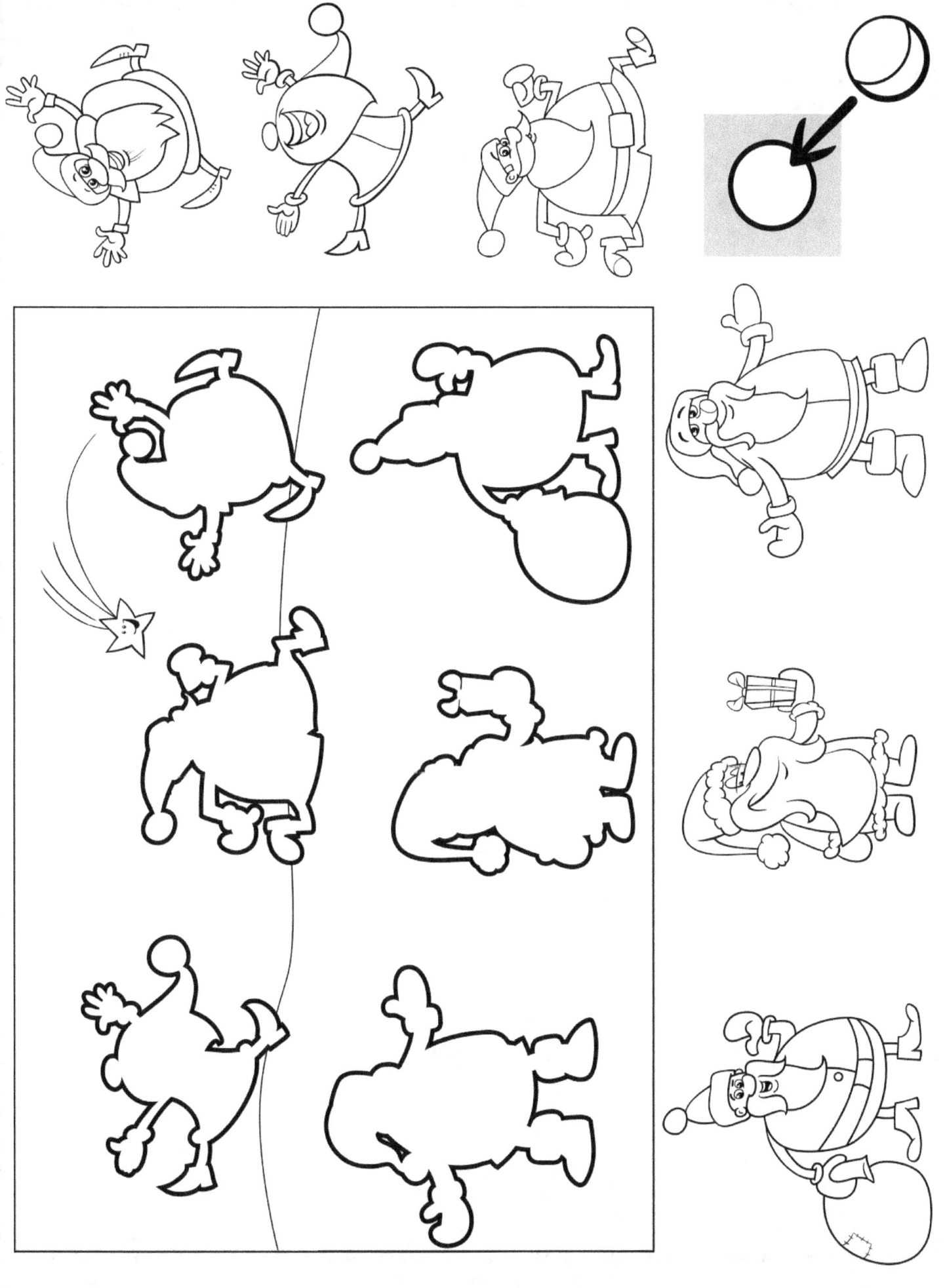

# WHAT COMES NEXT?

**1**

**2**

**3**

**4**

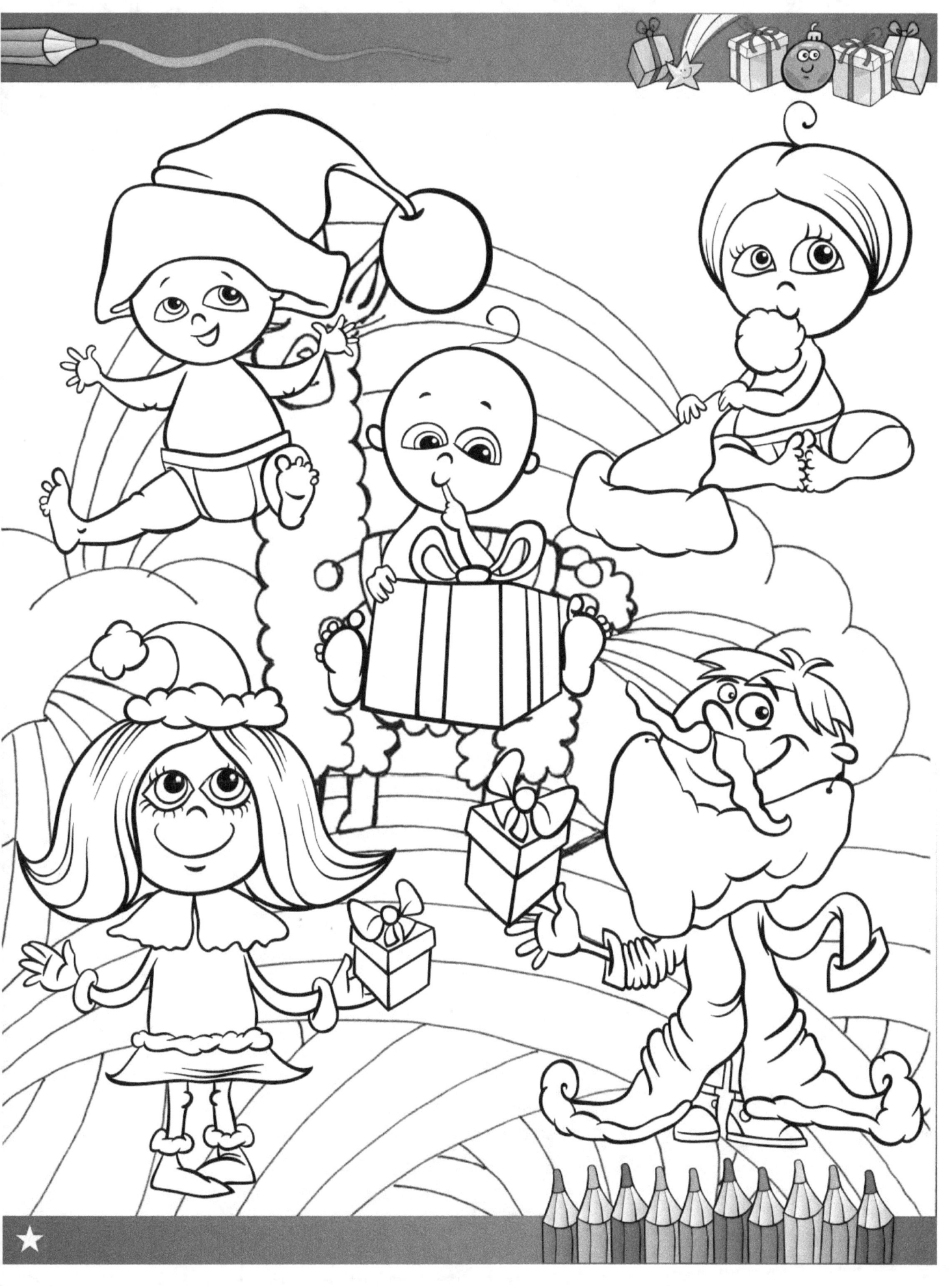

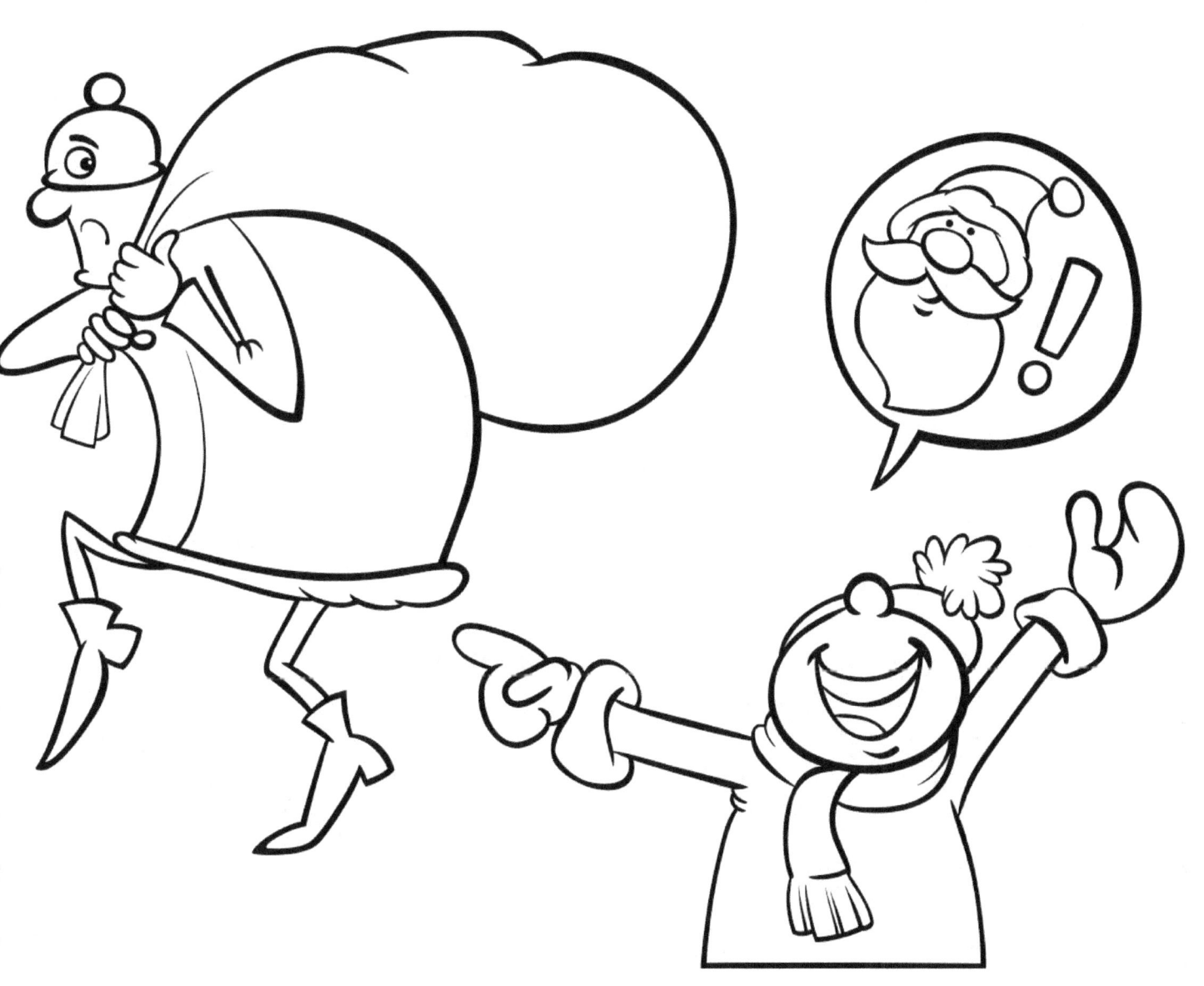

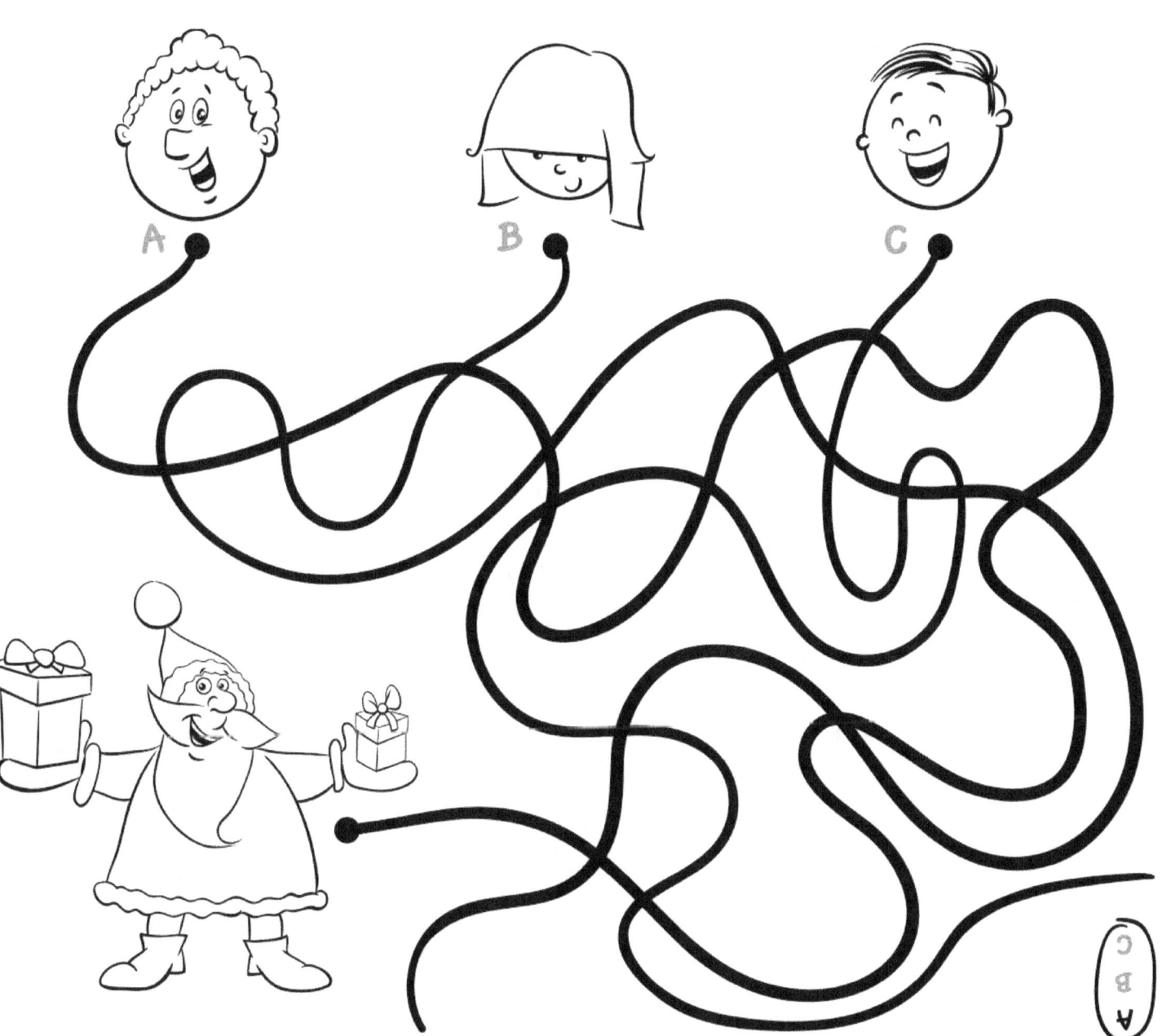

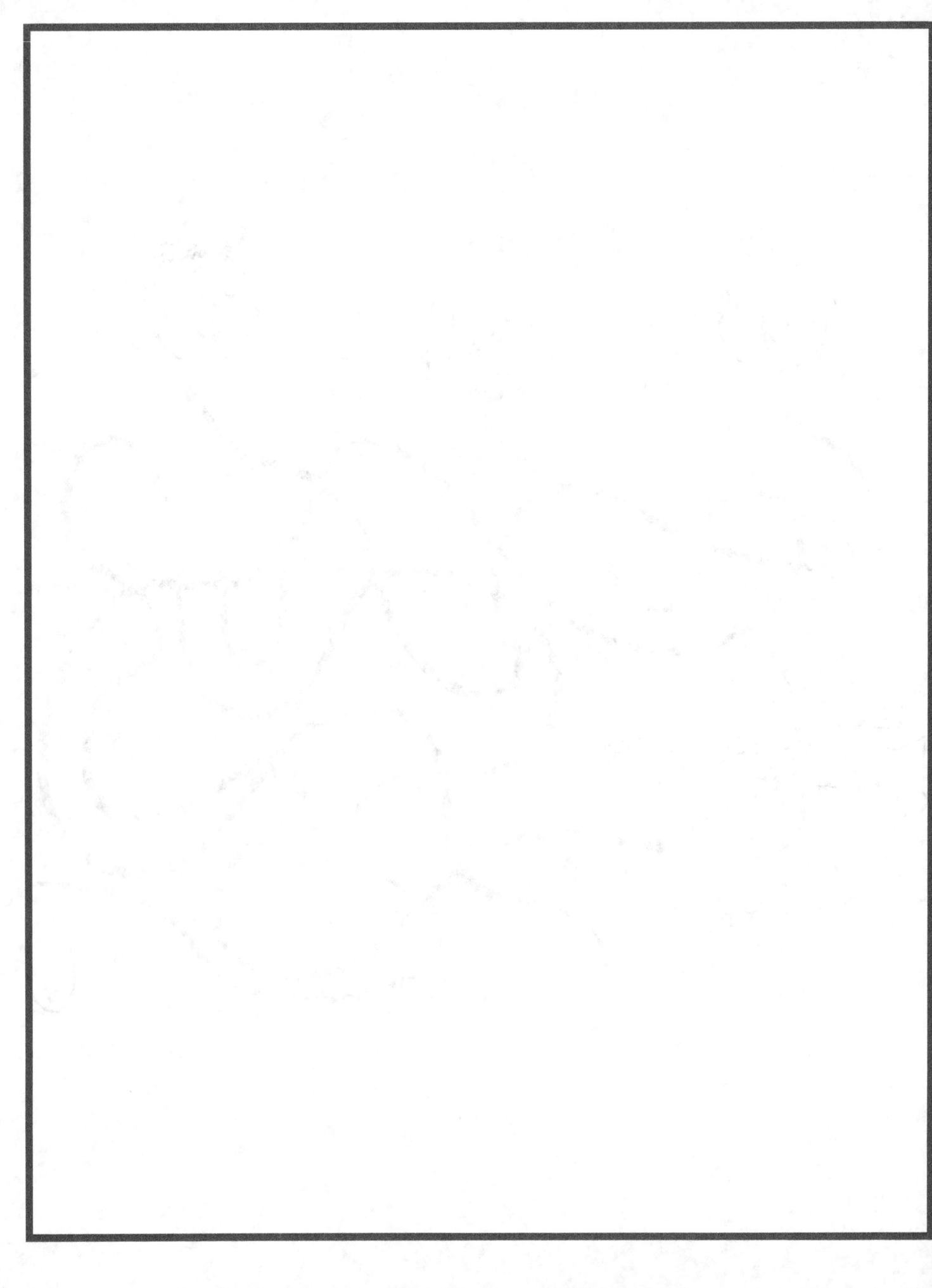

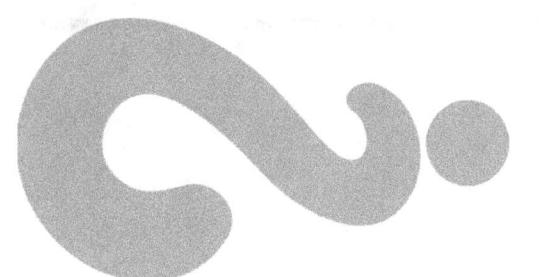

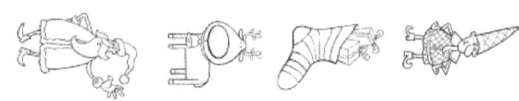

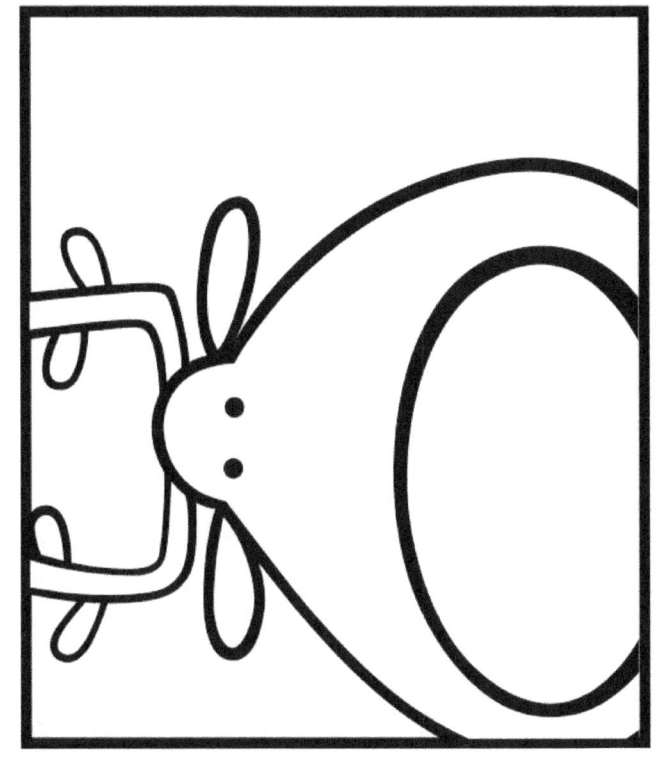

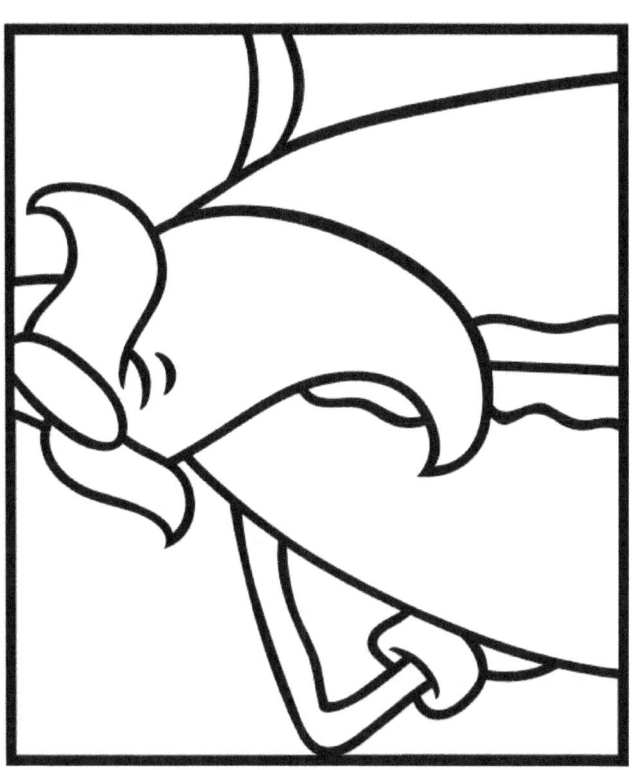

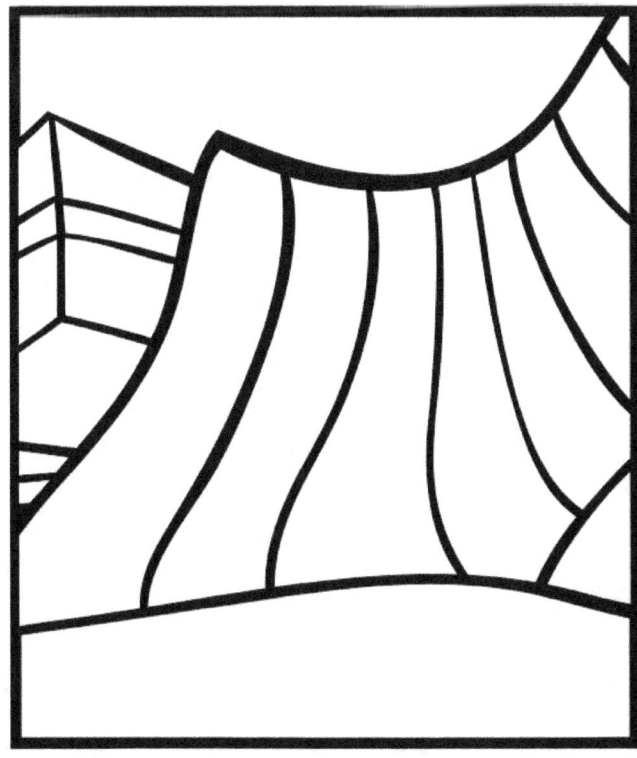

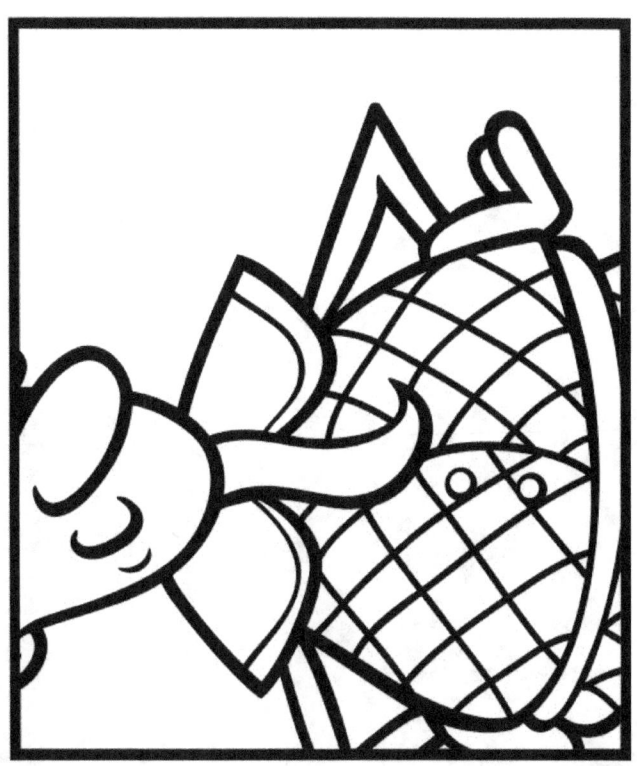

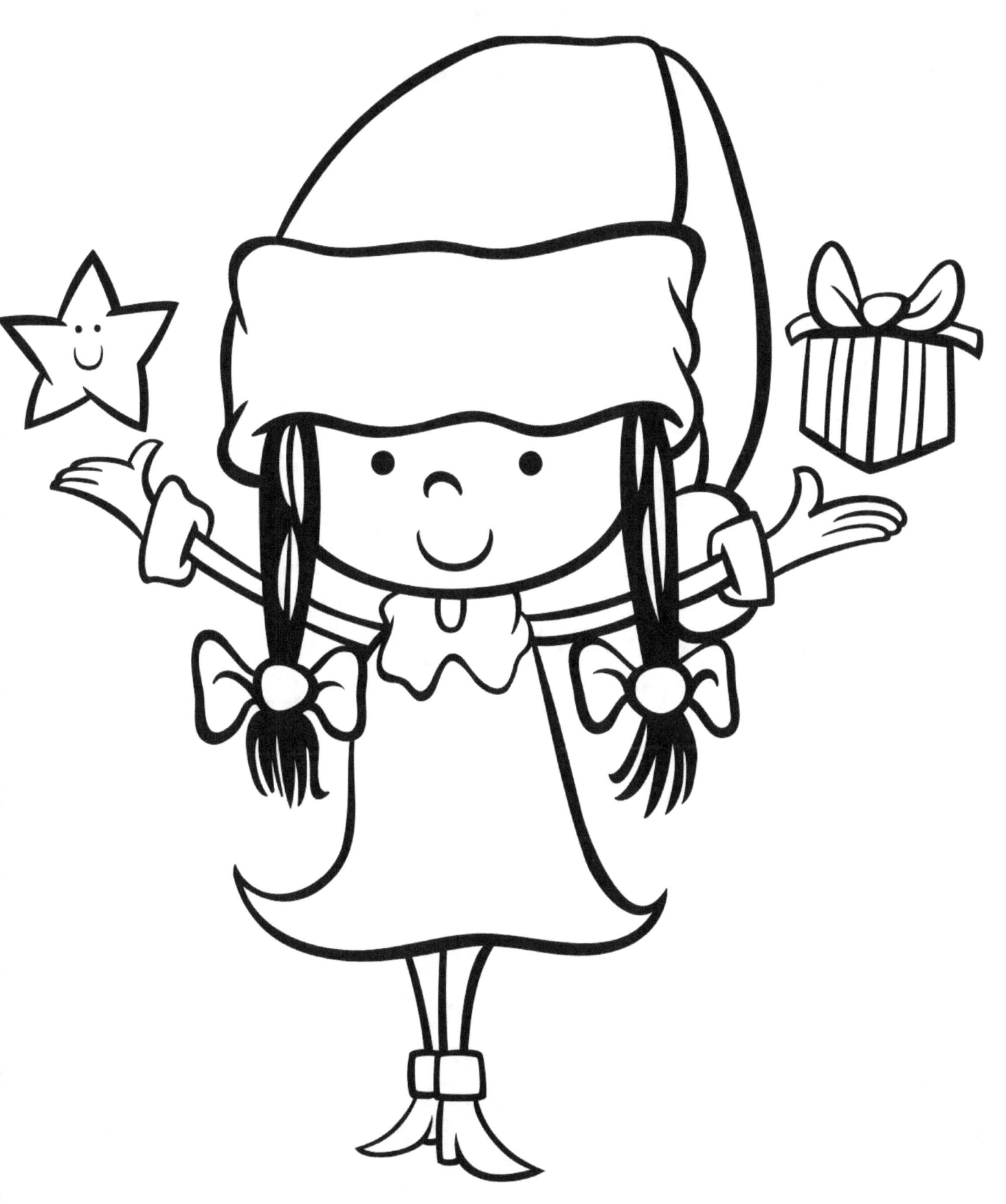

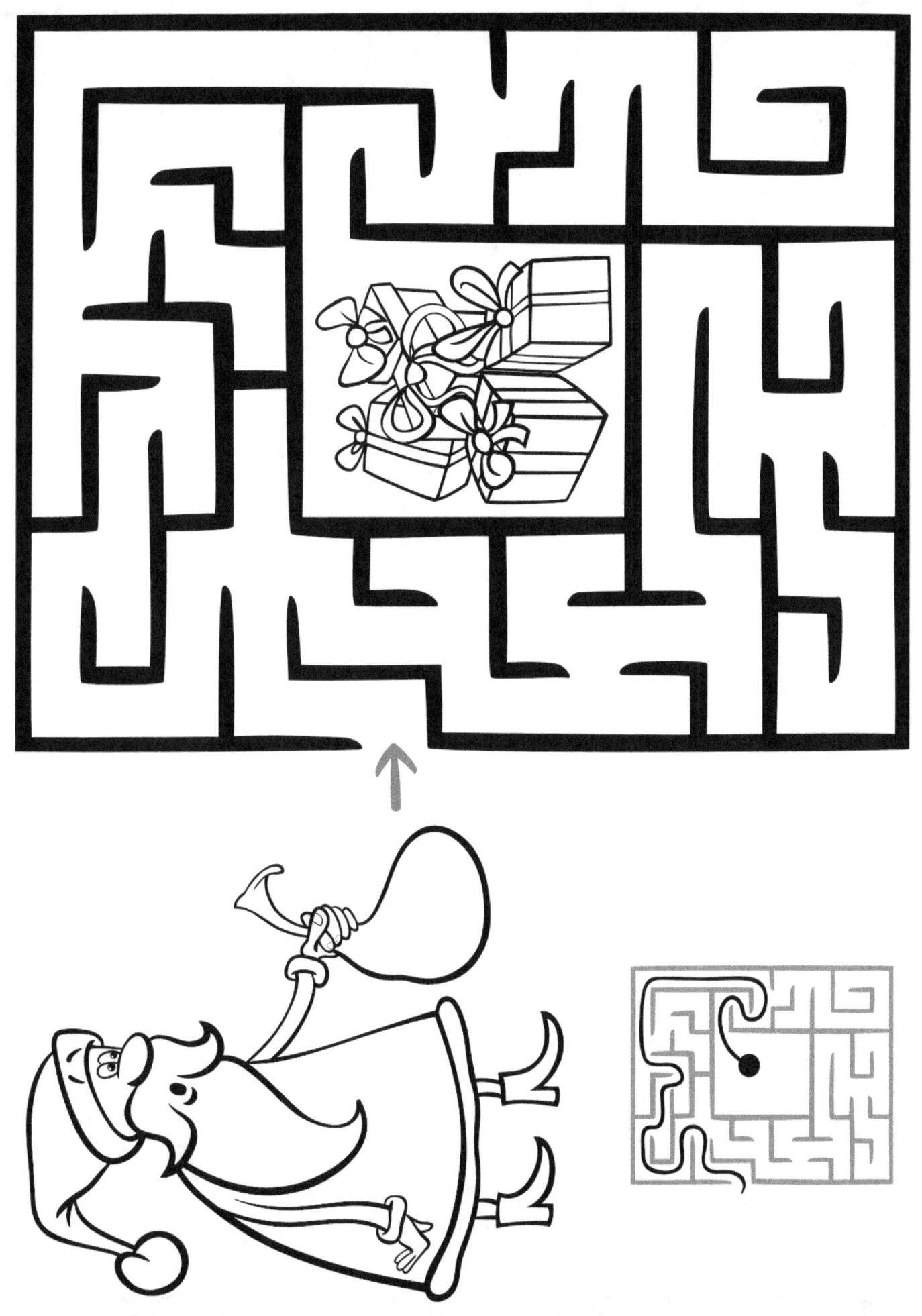

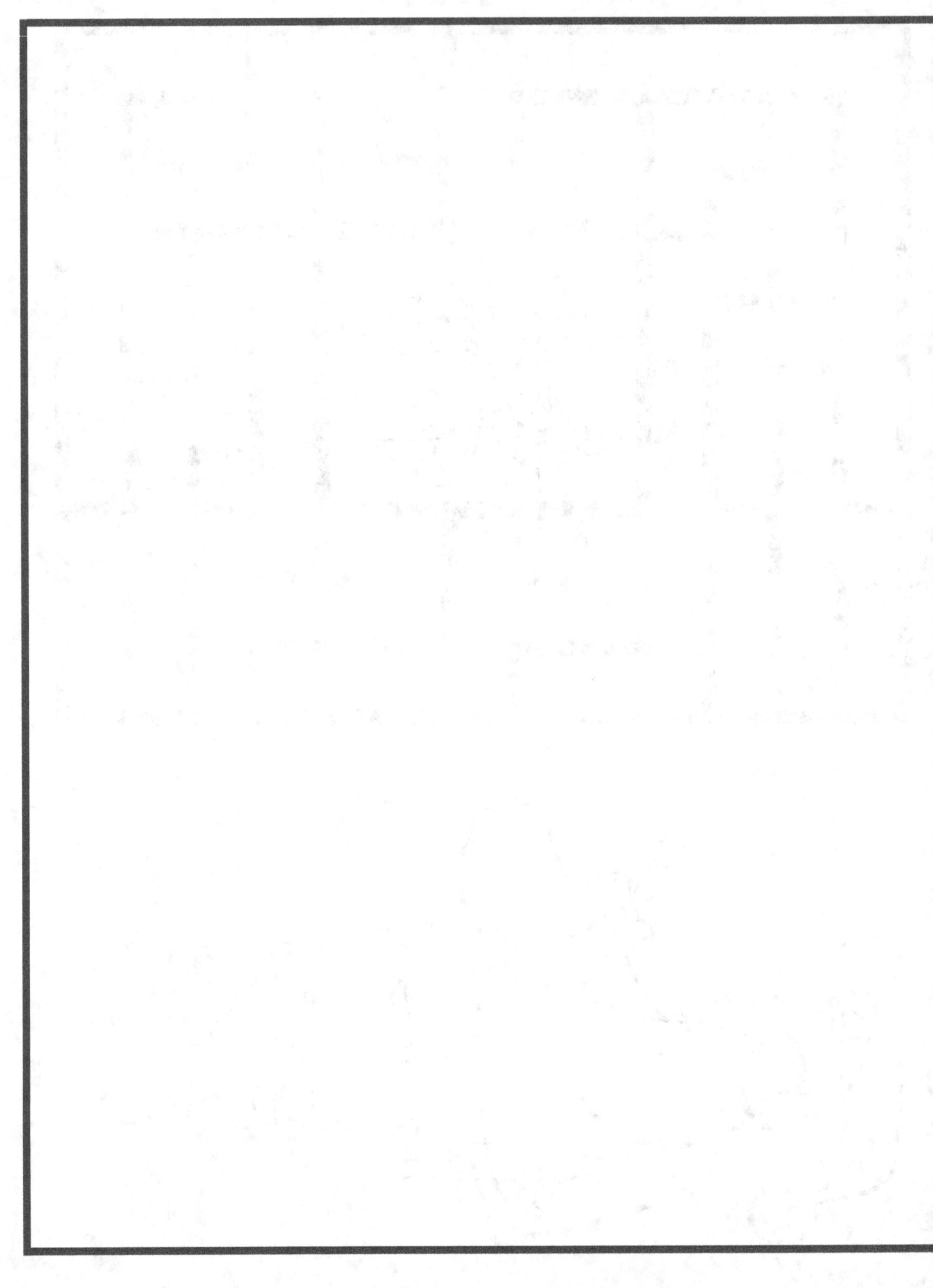

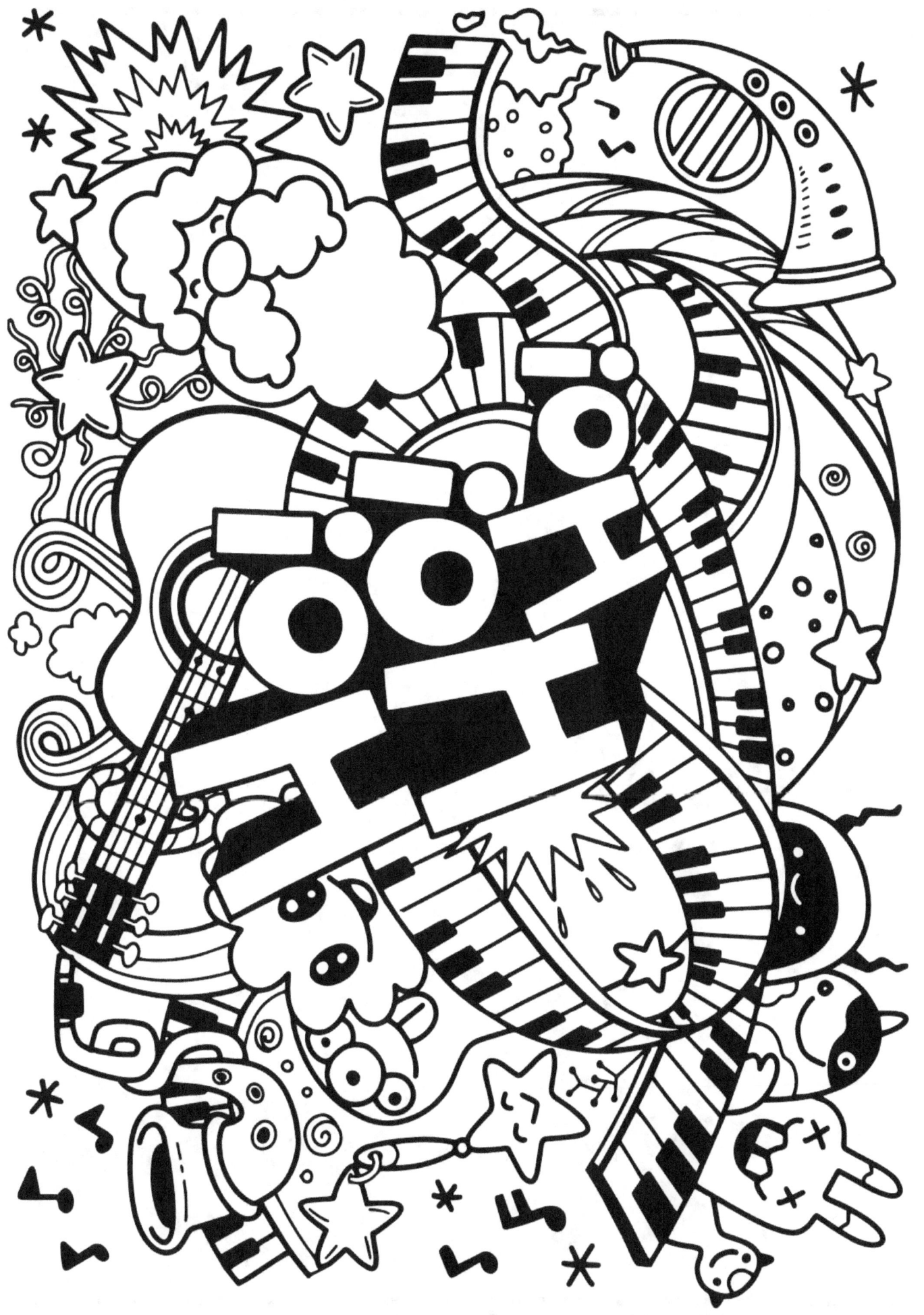

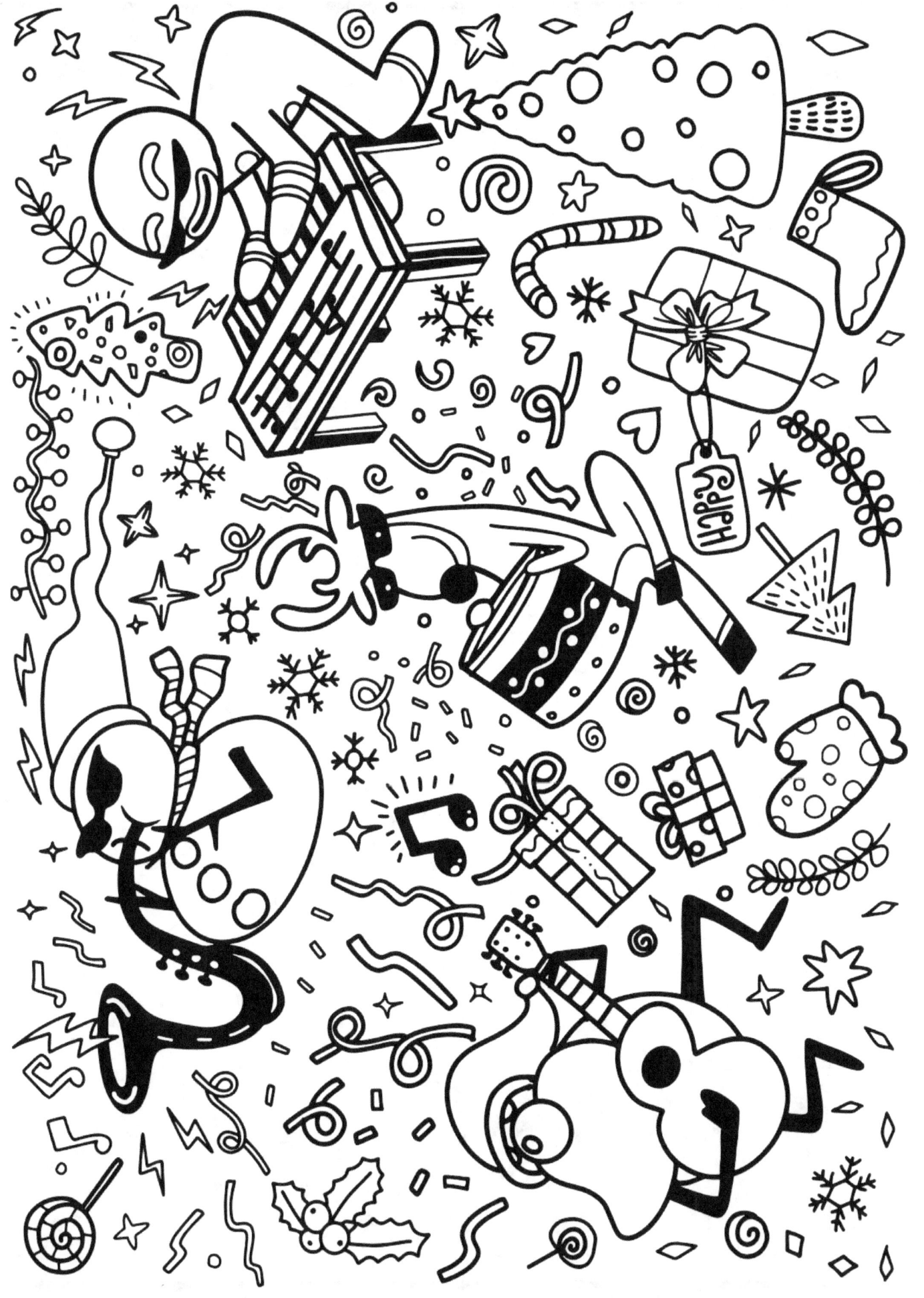

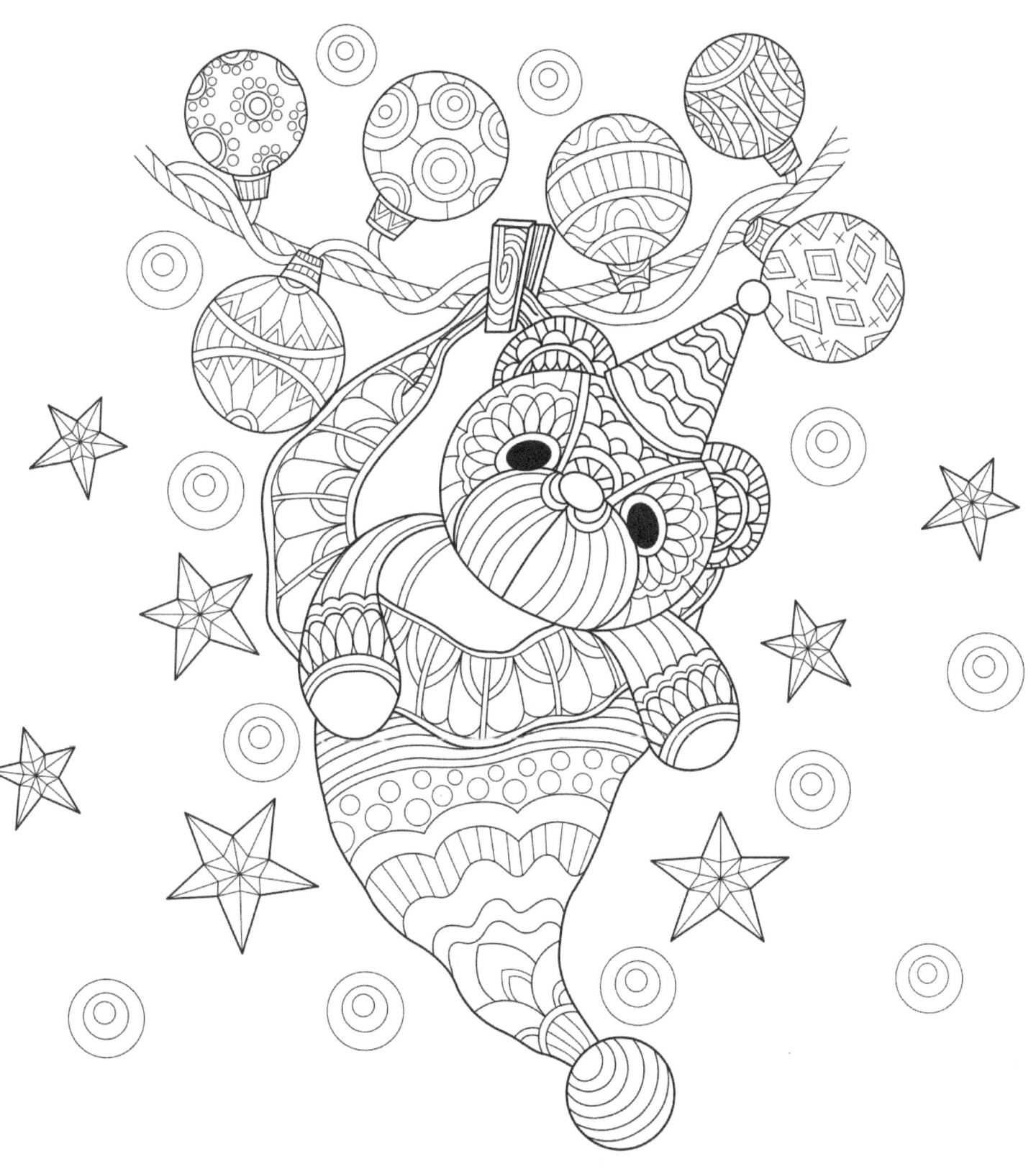

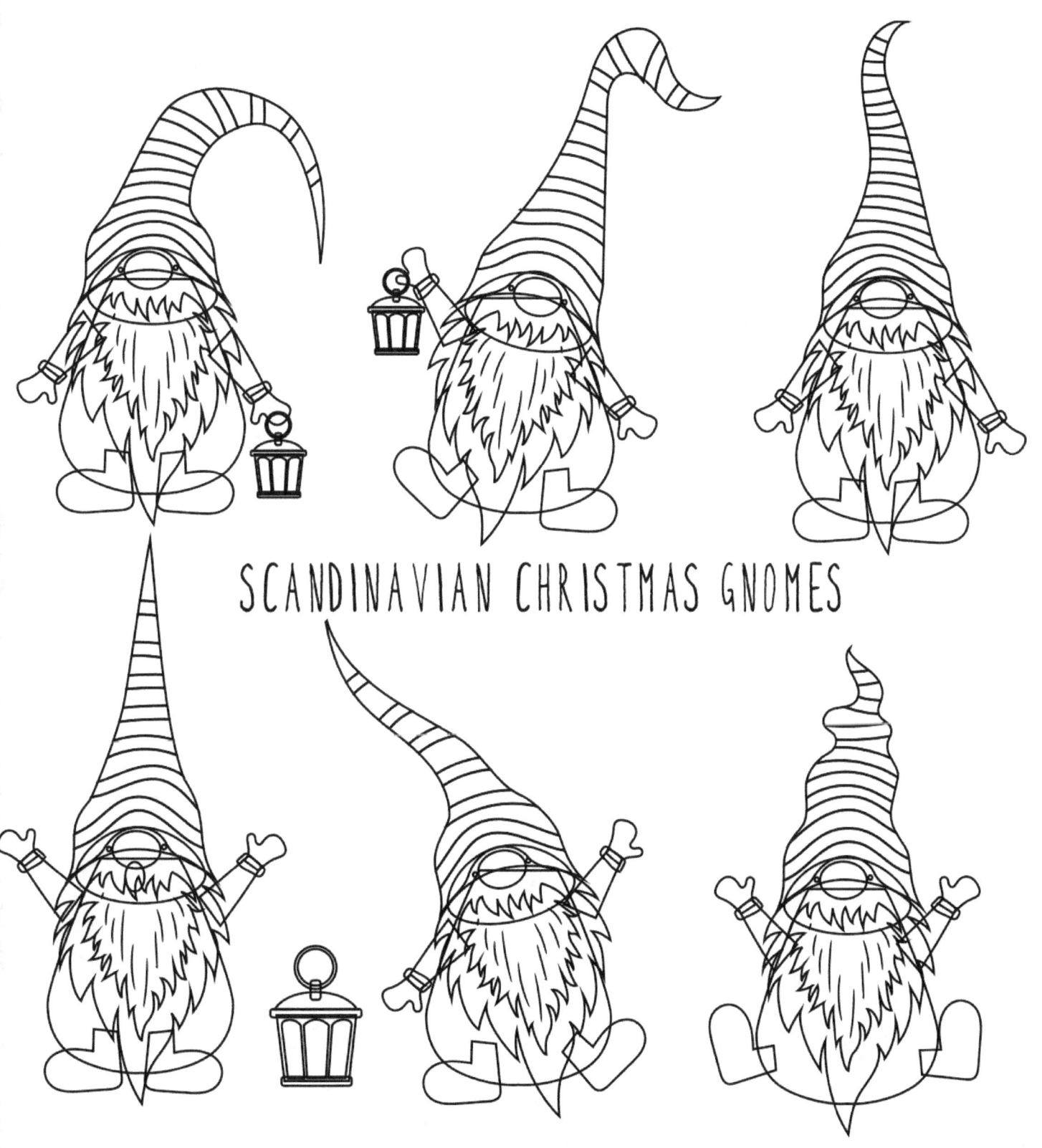

SCANDINAVIAN CHRISTMAS GNOMES

www.ingramcontent.com/pod-product-compliance
Lightning Source LLC
Chambersburg PA
CBHW081543220526

45467CB00010B/3312